101 Ideas for Embroidery on Paper

Erica Fortgens

SEARCH PRESS

CONTENTS

First published in Great Britain 2006 by Search Press Limited, Wellwood, North Farm Road, Tunbridge Wells, Kent TN2 3DR

Originally published in the Netherlands 2005 by Canticleer, an imprint of Tirion Uitgevers bv

Copyright © Tirion Uitgevers bv, Baarn

English translation by Mary Boorman in association with First Edition Translations Ltd, Cambridge

English translation copyright © Search Press Limited 2006

ISBN-10: 1-84448-192-1
ISBN-13: 978-1-84448-192-7

Suppliers

If you have any difficulty in obtaining any of the materials and equipment mentioned in this book, please visit the Search Press website for details of suppliers: www.searchpress.com Alternatively visit the author's website: www.ericafortgens.nl

I would like to thank Leonie Heuyerjans, Clasien Meester, Margriet Lugtmeier, Anneke Kaufman and Martha Daniels for all their assistance.

FOREWORD

In this extensive book you will find 101 cards that can be made by embroidery on paper – cards for all kinds of occasions, such as get well, birthday, new baby, Christmas, wedding, retirement, sympathy, first communion, congratulations and many more. It is an excellent reference book that includes a wide variety of patterns and designs so that, when browsing through, you are sure to find that certain something for a particular occasion. Embroidery on paper can be combined with other card techniques, so it is very versatile. You can, for example, combine it with embossing; cut-outs with Paperpatch paper behind them (a single sheet looks good but you can fold strips and overlap them); small beads; sparkles; and other decorative touches.

Each project contains a list of what to use for the various techniques but, for embroiderers out there, there are plenty of embroidery patterns to use without extra frills – it's up to you!

The combination of embroidery on card or paper with 3D embellishments is very attractive, and silk ribbon, bought in packs (or off the reel) adds another dimension. I have really enjoyed preparing this book and I hope that you, too, will get many hours of pleasure from it. Enjoy!

Erica Fortgens

MATERIALS

– Very fine Erica stylus with embroidery needle to suit
– Fine Erica stylus with embroidery needle to suit
– Coarse Erica stylus
– Erica mat for pricking
– Papicolor card
– Threads: Anchor Alcazar, Metallic, Reflect and Mouliné
– Masking tape, adhesive tape, adhesive
– Embossing materials: light box and tools
– Cutting mat and craft knife
– Erica's stencils
– Paperpatch paper
– Small scissors and 3D kit or foam

GENERAL METHOD

Order of work: pricking, embossing, cutting, embroidery, adding paper, finishing.

PRICKING

Copy the pattern or use a stencil: put it on the card, secure it with two strips of masking tape and place it on the mat. Prick the pattern through the card. Use the finest stylus for this. Use a larger stylus for holes that have to take several threads. Make sure that the hole is big enough. Hold the card up to the light to ensure that all the holes have been cleanly pricked. Carefully remove the pattern or the stencil. The pattern is now on the card.

Tip: always hold the stylus vertically.

EMBOSSING PARCHMENT

Place the stencil on the light box and secure it with masking tape. Place the card face down on the stencil and secure it with masking tape. Switch on the light box and press into the card with the embossing tool against the edge of the openings, gently at first and then applying more pressure.

Tip: First rub a little toilet soap over the part of the card to be embossed to make the embossing easier!

CUTTING

Secure the stencil to the card with masking tape. Put the whole piece of work on the cutting mat and cut along the edge of the openings, always on the same side; each time turn the whole piece on the cutting mat to make cutting easier.

EMBROIDERY

Follow the instructions step by step. For example put the needle through at A and leave about 2.5 cm (1 in) of thread at the back; secure it with a small piece of adhesive tape outside the area of the pattern pricked on the card.

THE NEEDLE

The needle must always be finer than the stylus. Use an appropriate size of needle. If you have a problem threading the needle, it might help to use a threading tool.

STEM STITCH

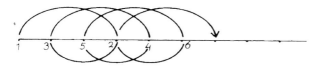

Work stem stitch as follows: 1–2 (2–3), 3–4 (4–5), 5–6 and so on. You always miss two holes on the right side and one on the underside. To make a smooth curve, embroider on the inside of the curve. If a curve doesn't work out perfectly, add an extra stitch; it is handwork after all!

PAPERPATCH

You can use pieces of Paperpatch paper behind the cut-out portions of the stencil, either as a single sheet or folded behind the cut-out. For this you can double over strips of about 2 cm (¾ in) (don't make the fold too sharp) and overlap the folded paper strips like roof tiles on the reverse of the card behind the opening. Fix them down with strips of adhesive tape.

Tip: Fix a piece of squared paper with masking tape on the front of the card so that it makes a temporary backing for the strips.

FINISHING

Finish off the card with strips of Papicolor, alternating with Paperpatch paper to tone with the card.

Get Well

1

MATERIALS

Papicolor card no. 29
3D sheet FK 1212
Thread: Alcazar yellow and green

Stitch from behind in the large holes and take the thread to the points as shown. Fix the 3D picture. Finish off the card in the same shades as the threads.

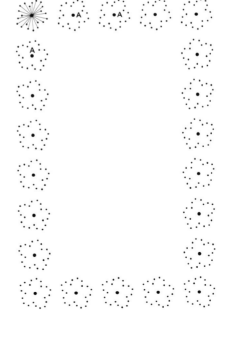

2

MATERIALS

Papicolor card no. 29
Embroidery template no. 4050 338
Thread: Anchor Alcazar metallic gold
3D sheet MB 0010

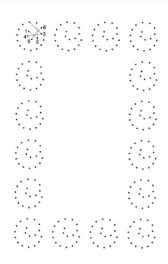

Prick the embroidery pattern through the card. Reverse the card and prick the decorative pattern through the card. Embroidery: stitch from behind in 1 and take the thread to 2; go along to 3 and take the thread to 4 and so on. Finish by attaching the 3D picture.

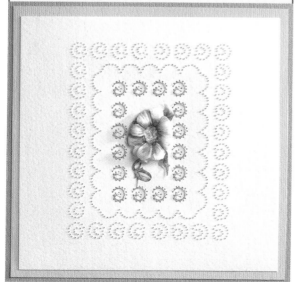

3

MATERIALS

Papicolor card no. 29
Threads: Alcazar yellow and dark green; Reflecta gold
3D step-by-step sheet no. 4008 099

Bring the thread forward through the large hole and take it to the points as shown. Finish by attaching the 3D flower.

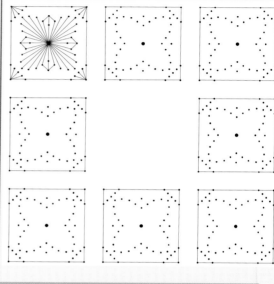

4

MATERIALS

Papicolor card no. 29
4.7 x 15.3 cm (1³/₄ x 6 in)
Erica's ruler for
embossing
Thread: Alcazar
metallic gold

Embroider the drops in gold and take the thread to the points as shown. Embroider the loops in stem stitch.

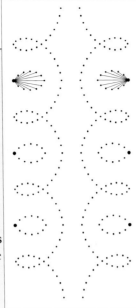

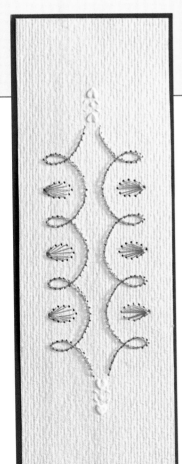

5

MATERIALS

Embroidery kit rose no. 4050 115

Embroider the flower drops as previously. Attach the 3D picture.

6

MATERIALS

Embroidery kit silk ribbon blue no. 4050 116

Embroidery: bring the thread through the large hole and take to the points as shown previously. To make the ribbon roses make a spider's web and then weave the ribbon through it. Finish off the card.

7

MATERIALS

Papicolor card no. 27
Allure stencil no. 4050 310
Thread: Alcazar moss green
3D step-by-step sheet no. 4008 099

Use the stencil to prick out the pattern. Embroidery: embroider all the triangles with double thread to cover well. Attach the 3D picture.

8

MATERIALS

Erica's pink parchment paper
Papicolor double card no. 25
Erica's stencil no. 4050 510
Thread: Anchor Mouliné pale pink and
    dark pink

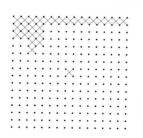

Prick the pattern through the parchment paper. Cut out the frame. Do the embossing. Embroidery: use cross-stitch in pale pink and dark pink thread.

8

9

MATERIALS

Erica's light blue parchment paper
Papicolor card no. 19
Stencils no. 4050 301 (geometric) and
no. 4050 305 (frame)
Threads: Anchor Mouliné pale blue and
dark blue

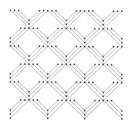

Cut out the frame in the card using stencils. Find the centre of the card with two intersecting diagonal pencil lines so you know where to cut again. Embroider the stitches of the pattern with a double strand of silk.

10

MATERIALS

Erica's silk ribbon square template no.
4050 341
Paperpatch yellow no. 4050 809
Silk yellow ribbon 4 mm (¼ in)
Bodkin
Papicolor card no. 29, 3 x 3 cm
(1¼ x 1¼ in)

Use the silk ribbon template to embroider the spider's web for the flower on the small card. Weave the silk ribbon through the web; stitch through from behind and make loops with the ribbon through the web. Finish with Paperpatch paper.

Valentine

11

MATERIALS

Papicolor card no. 29
Thread: Alcazar metallic gold
3D step-by-step sheet no. 4008 099

Bring the thread through the large hole from
the back to the points as shown. Attach the
3D tulip.

12

MATERIALS

Papicolor card in various shades of pink: nos. 25, 42, 13
Paperpatch pink no. 4050 802

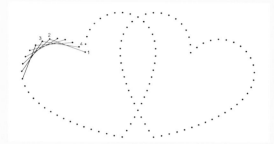

Embroidery: Bring the thread through at 1 and take it to 2; go behind to 3 and draw the thread to 4, and so on, until you have embroidered half the heart. Begin again on the other side of the heart. Finish off with Paperpatch paper.

13

MATERIALS

Papicolor card 9 x 9 cm (3¾ x 3¾ in)
Thread: Anchor Alcazar light pink
3D sheet MB 0020

Bring the thread from the back through the large hole to the points as shown. Attach the 3D flower to the card.

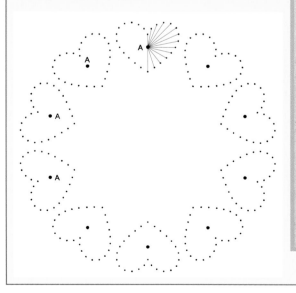

Birthday

14

MATERIALS

Papicolor card no. 27
Erica geometric stencil
    no. 4050 301
Thread: Alcazar dark green;
    Reflecta gold
Small gold beads
Paperpatch gold no. 4050 805

Prick out the design and then
do the embossing.
Leaves: Bring the thread
through the large hole from
the back to the points as
shown. Embroider the stems
in stem stitch. Stitch the petals
of the flowers in gold. Attach the beads.
Vase: put the pattern on the back of the
Paperpatch paper and prick the points of the
corners. Draw the lines from point to point
with pencil and ruler. Cut out the vase and
attach it with adhesive to the card. Outline
with stitches in Reflecta gold thread.

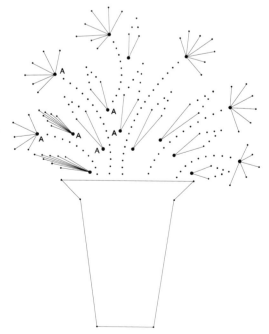

MATERIALS

Papicolor card pink no. 25, 6.5 x 6.5 cm
   (2½ x 2½ in)
Silk ribbon in various shades of pink
Thread: Alcazar light green
Paperpatch pink no. 4050 802
Template for silk ribbon embroidery
   no. 4050 341
Bodkin and small gold beads

Prick out the embroidery pattern and the three spider's webs using the template. Leaves: bring the thread through from the large hole to the points. Roses: embroider the spider's webs and weave the silk ribbon through. Always make a new loop. Attach beads with thread and secure at back. Finish with Paperpatch paper.

MATERIALS

Papicolor card no. 27
Thread: Reflecta gold
3D step-by-step sheet no. 4008 098

Embroider the text in stem stitch (here only pass over 1 hole) on a card 12 x 2 cm (4½ x ¾ in). Attach the 3D picture. Stick the strip with the text onto a dark red card and attach this diagonally at the top corner of the card; cut off surplus paper at the edges of the card.

17

MATERIALS

Papicolor card no. 27
Thread: Reflecta gold
3D step-by-step sheet no. 4008 098

Embroider the text in stem stitch
(only pass over 1 hole here) and make
a label.
Attach the 3D picture of the teddy bear.

18

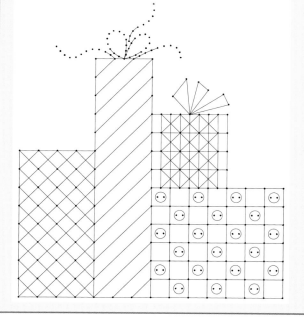

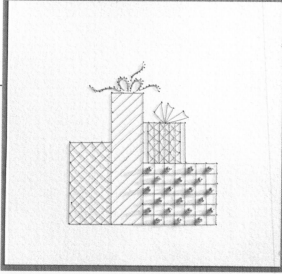

MATERIALS

Papicolor card no. 27
Thread: Alcazar metallic gold
Small gold beads

Embroider all straight lines as shown.
Ribbon: use stem stitch. Attach the beads as
shown. Finish off the card.

19

MATERIALS

Papicolor card pink no. 25
Erica stencil no. 4050 308
Threads: Alcazar various shades of pink and soft green

After pricking the design, do the embossing. Embroider the leaves and flowers: pull the thread through the large hole from the back and take to the points as shown. Large flower: bring thread through 1 and take to 2; go behind to 3 and take to 4, and so on.

20

MATERIALS

Papicolor card no. 20
Paperpatch gold no. 4050 801
Thread: Alcazar metallic pale gold

Embroider the whole design in stem stitch. Finish off with a piece of Paperpatch paper.

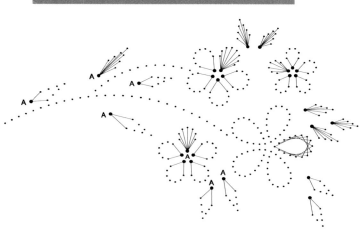

MATERIALS

Papicolor card no. 27
Thread: Reflecta gold

Embroider the orange slices in stem stitch. Embroider the glasses with straight stitches from point to point. Bubbles in the glasses: make a knot in the thread, pull the thread through the card from front to back, fix it and clip the thread from the top of the knot.

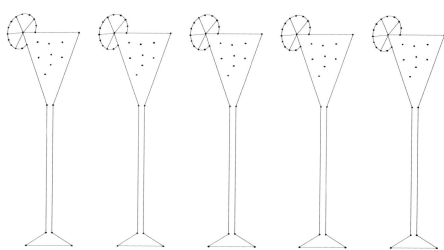

22

MATERIALS

Papicolor card nos. 25 and 22
Thread: Alcazar two shades of pink and pale green

Tulip flowers: bring the needle from the back through the big hole and take the thread to the points as shown. Embroider the leaves in the same way. Stems: use stem stitch.

23

MATERIALS

Papicolor card no. 43
3D sheet MB 0009
Thread: Alcazar metallic gold

Embroidery: use stem stitch for the border. Attach the 3D picture.

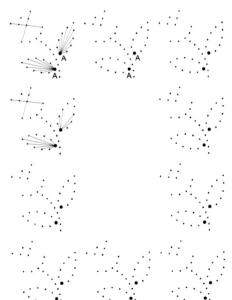

First Communion

MATERIALS

Papicolor card no. 42
Thread: Alcazar blue and Reflecta gold

Embroider in cross-stitch as shown.

New Home

25

MATERIALS

Papicolor card no. 17
Green and yellow
    paper
Sheet no. 4050 953 for
    the flowers

Key: embroider in stem stitch, taking the thread from point to point on the straight lines with a long stitch. Attach the flower picture.

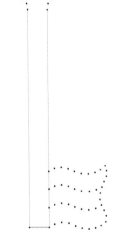

26

MATERIALS

Papicolor card no. 17
Thread: Alcazar green
Silk ribbon green
    and gold

Embroider the leaves: bring thread through the large hole from the back to the points as shown. Stems: use stem stitch. Ribbon flowers: bring ribbon through from back of card and knot it, then take it back through the second hole. Make the other flowers in the same way.

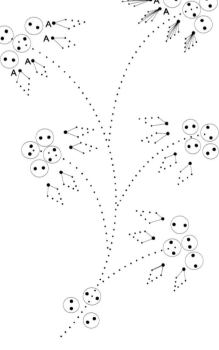

Anniversary

27

MATERIALS

Papicolor dark blue card no. 41

Thread: Alcazar metallic gold

Numeral 25: embroider in stem stitch. Scrolls: Bring the thread from the back at 1 and take it to 2; go behind to 3 and then take it to 4, and so on, until the shape is complete.

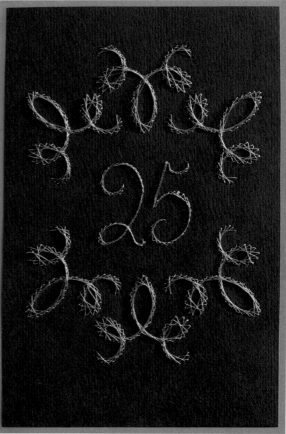

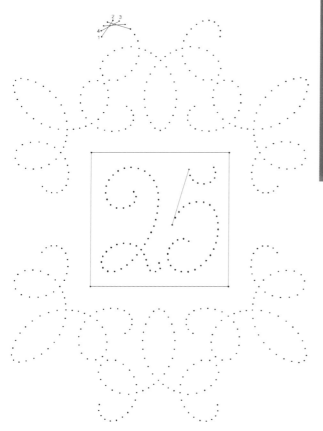

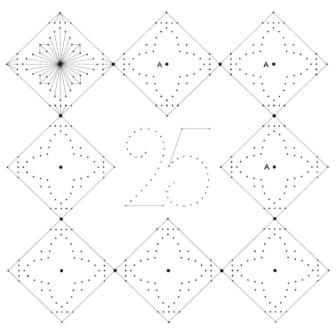

MATERIALS

Papicolor card no. 42
Thread: Alcazar blue and Reflecta gold

Numeral 25: embroider in stem stitch.
Squares: bring the thread through the
large hole from the back and take it to
the points as shown. Outline the
squares with Reflecta gold.

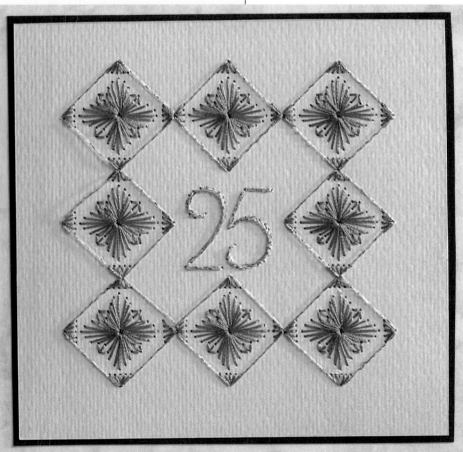

New Baby

29

MATERIALS

Papicolor pink card no. 25
Baby sheet no. 4050 952
Thread: Alcazar pink and Reflecta gold
3D foam

Embroidery: bring the thread through the large hole from the back to the points as shown. Outline the straight lines with Reflecta gold. Cut out the corners and the picture. Attach the teddy bear on 3D foam. Attach the corners with adhesive.

30

MATERIALS

Papicolor card no. 42, 8 x 8 cm
  (3 x 3 in)
Thread: Alcazar pale blue;
  Reflecta gold
Baby sheet no. 4050 951
3D foam

Embroider the corners: bring
the thread from the back
through the large hole and take
it to the points as shown. Stitch
the straight lines with Reflecta
gold. Cut out the picture and
attach it to 3D foam and fix to
the card. Attach the corners
with adhesive.

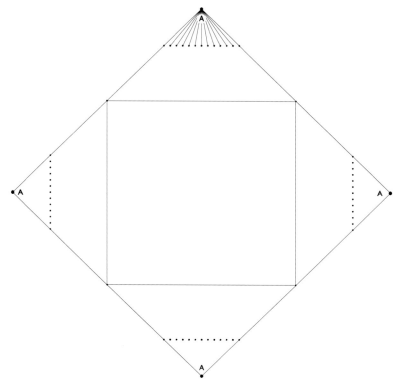

31

MATERIALS

Papicolor paper in three shades of pink: nos. 22, 25, 34
Sheet no. 4050 952
Small gold beads
Thread: Reflecta gold

Embroider the text in stem stitch on a card slightly bigger than the cut-out border. Fix the border on the card and trim the edge to leave a small border. Attach the label to a larger card. Thread a bead chain and fix it to the label.

32

MATERIALS

Papicolor card in two shades of pink: nos. 25 and 34
Thread: Reflecta gold
3D foam

Embroider the ribbon in stem stitch. Place label on 3D foam and attach to card with a bead chain.

33

MATERIALS

Papicolor card no. 19 and Spectra blue no. 06
Thread: Reflecta gold
Teddy bear sheet no. 4050 951

Embroider the cross-stitch border and outline the straight lines with Reflecta gold. Attach the picture to blue paper and fix it in the square.

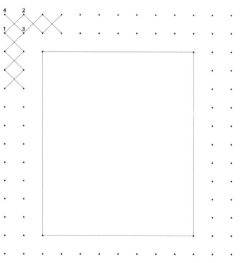

34

MATERIALS

Papicolor card no. 27
Thread: Reflecta gold
3D step-by-step sheet no. 4008 098
Gold paper

Embroider as follows: bring the thread through the large hole and take to the points as shown. Attach the 3D pictures.

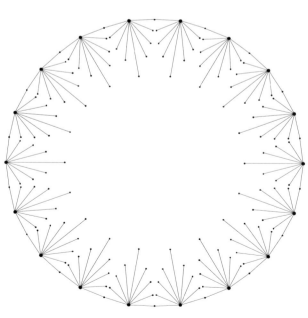

35

MATERIALS

Papicolor card no. 34
Label sheet 4050 952
Thread: Alcazar dark pink
3D foam

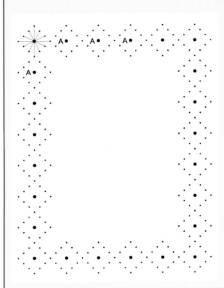

Embroider on a pink card 7 x 5 cm (3 x 2 in). Bring the thread through the large hole from the back and take to the points as shown.

Cut out the text and fix it to a small pink card. Trim the edges and attach it to the card on 3D foam. Finish off the card.

36

MATERIALS

Papicolor card no. 10
Duck multi stencil no. 4050 340
Embossing material
Paperpatch yellow no. 4050 809

Place the stencil diagonally on the card and prick the holes for the embroidered border through the card. Cut out the duck. Do the embossing.

Embroider the border. Fold strips of Paperpatch paper and overlap them behind the cut-out duck.

Nature

37

MATERIALS

Papicolor card no. 27
Thread: Alcazar orange
Pastel crayons in three shades, pink, yellow
    and orange

Embroider the butterflies in stem stitch. Colour the
wings gently with the pastel crayons. Rub smooth with a
finger. Remove surplus colour with a rubber.

38

MATERIALS

Papicolor card pink nos. 25 and 22
Thread: Alcazar metallic gold
Embroidery stencil no. 4050 338

Prick the pattern for the butterflies through
the card. Turn the card over, fix it to the
stencil and prick the two border patterns
through the card. Finish off the card.

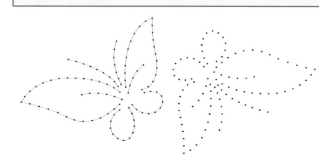

39

MATERIALS

Papicolor pink card no. 25
Silk ribbon cream and pale green
Thread: Alcazar pale green

Embroider the leaves: bring the thread through the large hole from the back and take to the points as shown. Stems: use stem stitch. Silk ribbon flowers: put the ribbon through one of the holes and tie a knot at the front (or two depending on the width of the ribbon) and put the end through the second hole to the back of the card.

40

MATERIALS

Papicolor round card natural no. 56
Green paper
Thread: Alcazar green and Alcazar metallic gold
Silk ribbon green and cream

Embroider the leaves: bring the thread through the large hole and take to the points. Stems and outline of the dove: use stem stitch. Wing: bring the thread through at 1 and take to 2; go along to 3 and take the thread to 4, and so on, until you have completed the wing. Silk ribbon nest: bring ribbon through to the front, make a knot and push the end back through the other hole.

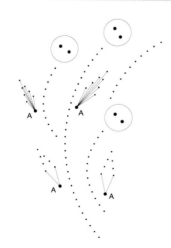

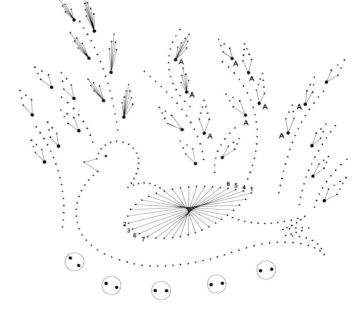

41

MATERIALS

Papicolor card natural no. 55
Erica stencil no. 4050 510
Embossing material
Thread: Alcazar two shades of brown

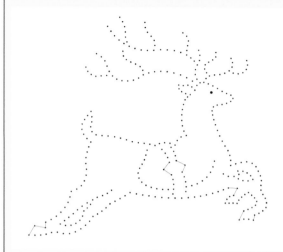

Prick the pattern through the card. Emboss the border. Embroider the stag in stem stitch, passing over only 1 hole; this makes the outline neater.

42

MATERIALS

Papicolor card no. 02
Thread: Alcazar metallic gold
Small gold beads

Make the fins and the tail of the fish as follows: bring the thread through 1 and take it to 2; go behind to 3 and bring it out at 4 until the triangle has been worked. Take a thread along the gaps. Eyes: make a knot in the thread and take it through the card from the front. Attach the beads with a stitch.

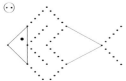

43

MATERIALS

Papicolor card no. 34
Thread: Anchor Mouliné blue and orange; Reflecta gold
Small gold beads

Instructions: see card 42.

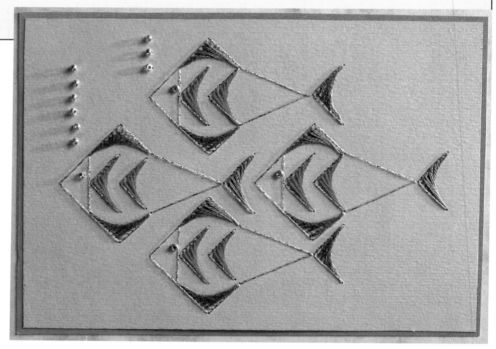

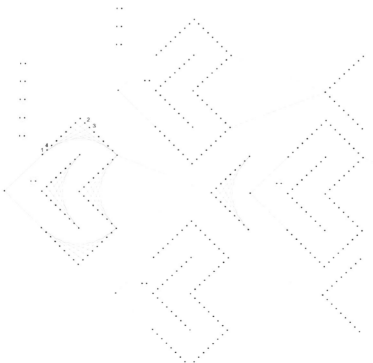

Christmas

MATERIALS

Papicolor card no. 27
Thread: Alcazar metallic gold
Sparkles no. 4009 103

Embroider the card following
the drawing. Lower part: bring
the thread through the large
hole and take it to the points as
shown. Embroider the crosses.
Take a long stitch to outline the
candle. Attach the sparkles as
shown in the illustration.

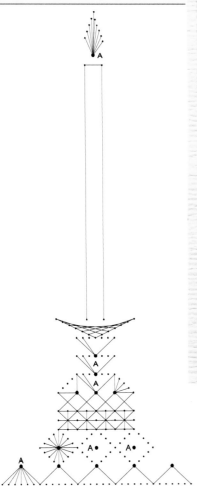

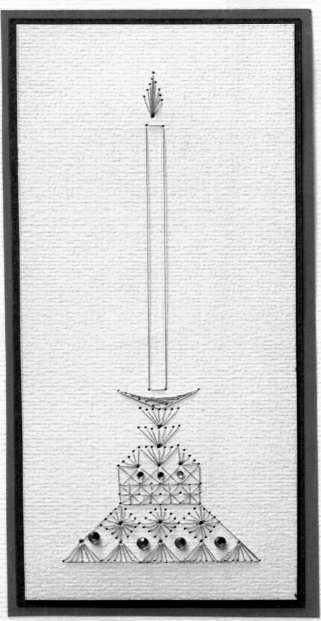

MATERIALS

Papicolor card no. 19
Erica stencil frame no. 4050 305
Thread: Anchor Mouliné soft green; Reflecta gold

Do the pricking and then the embossing. Embroider the tree as follows: bring the thread through the large hole and take it to the points as shown. Outline with lines of Reflecta gold. Work the candles in Reflecta gold.

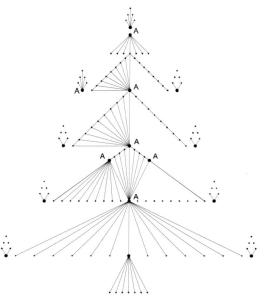

MATERIALS

Papicolor card no. 27
Thread: Alcazar pale green; Reflecta gold

Embroidery: bring the thread through the large hole and take to the points as shown. Outline the tree with a thread of Reflecta gold.

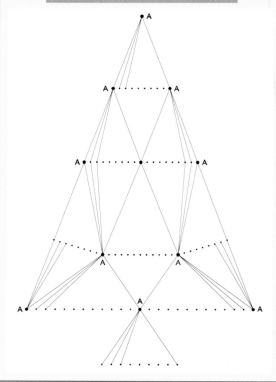

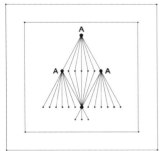
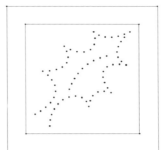
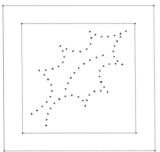
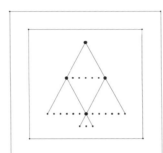

MATERIALS

Papicolor cards no. 27, 4.5 x 4.5 cm
  (1³/₄ x 1³/₄ in)
Thread: Reflecta gold, Alcazar dark green

Tree: bring the thread through the large hole and bring to the points as shown. Outline with Reflecta gold. Holly leaf: use stem stitch. Outline the four squares with Reflecta gold.

MATERIALS

Papicolor card no. 27
Thread: Alcazar red, blue; Reflecta gold
Silk ribbon for the bows

Embroidery: Stitch all the lines as shown on the drawing. Make pretty bows on the parcels.

49

MATERIALS

Papicolor card no. 18
Red silk ribbon and small red beads

Make the wreath with the silk ribbon. Each time pull the ribbon through, make one or two knots and take the end through to the back. Loosely secure the knots with a bead. Make a pretty bow.

50

MATERIALS

Papicolor card no. 27
Thread: Alcazar metallic gold

Embroider the square panes; bring the thread through from the back at 1 and take to 2; go behind to 3 and take to 4 and so on until you have worked the square. Stitch the straight lines. Curves: use stem stitch.

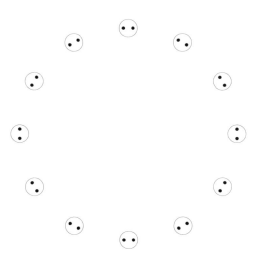

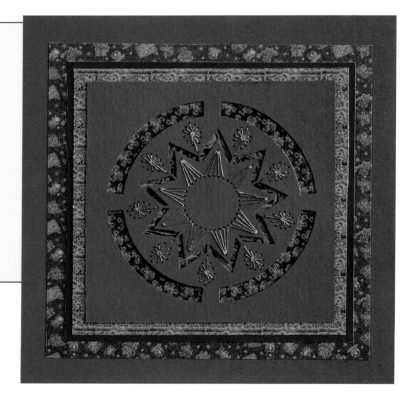

51

MATERIALS

Papicolor card no. 43
Erica stencil no. 4050 312
Thread: Alcazar metallic gold
Paperpatch red no. 4050 806

Prick out the pattern on the card. Cut out the star and the round frame. Embroider the card as shown. Fix the Paperpatch paper behind the card with adhesive.

52

MATERIALS

Papicolor card no. 27
Erica stencil no. 4050 312
Thread: Alcazar metallic gold
Paperpatch gold no. 4050 801

Use the stencil to prick out the pattern and then do the embossing. Embroidery: bring the thread through the large hole and take to the points as shown. Cut out a label and finish off the card with the gold Paperpatch paper.

53

MATERIALS

Papicolor card no.27
Erica stencil Bethlehem no. 4050 314
Thread: Alcazar metallic gold
Paperpatch gold no. 4050 805

Prick the pattern through the card using the stencil. Do the embossing. Embroidery: make the stitches of the stars as shown. Finish card with Paperpatch paper.

55

MATERIALS

Papicolor card no. 27
Erica multi-stencil no. 4050 330
Thread: Alcazar metallic gold
Paperpatch gold no. 4050 805

Cut out the star shape from the card using the stencil. Turn the card over and prick the decorative pattern on the card. Prick the holes for the stitches and outline the star. Fold strips of gold Paperpatch paper and overlap behind the opening. Finish off the card with more of the Paperpatch.

54

MATERIALS

Papicolor card no. 41
Erica multi-stencil bell no. 4050 329
Paperpatch blue no. 4050 808

Cut out the bell with the help of the stencil. Overlap strips of Paperpatch paper behind the holes. Finish off the card with more of the Paperpatch.

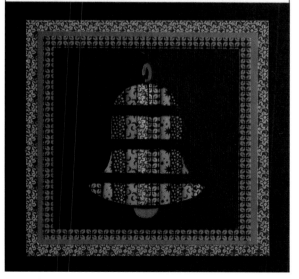

56

MATERIALS

Papicolor card no. 27
Erica multi-stencil angel no. 4050 328
Thread: Alcazar metallic gold
Paperpatch gold no. 4050 805

Prick the pattern through the card. Do the embossing. Embroider the pattern as shown. Finish off the card with Paperpatch paper.

57

MATERIALS

Papicolor card no. 43
Erica multi-stencil tree no. 4050 327
Paperpatch green no. 4050 807
Thread: Alcazar metallic gold

Cut out the tree using the stencil.
Prick the holes for the embroidery: work the cross-stitch, candles and the flames. Fold strips of the Paperpatch paper and overlap them behind the holes. Use more to finish off the card.

58

MATERIALS

Papicolor card no. 27
Embroidery stencil for candlestick no. 4050 332
Thread: Alcazar metallic

Use the stencil to prick out the pattern for the embroidery. Turn the card over and prick out the decorative pattern. Embroider the candles as shown.

MATERIALS

Papicolor card no. 27
Thread: Alcazar soft green
3D sheet MB 0029

Make a large enough hole in the centre of the tree with the stylus. Bring the thread through and take it to the points as shown. Repeat for all the trees. Attach the 3D picture.

MATERIALS

Papicolor card no. 41
3D sheet MB 0030
Thread: Alcazar metallic gold; Reflecta gold

Embroider the stars as shown. Alternate the metallic and the Reflecta thread. Attach the 3D picture.

61

MATERIALS

Papicolor card no. 27
Erica embroidery stencil no. 4050 331
Thread: Alcazar metallic gold

Prick the pattern though the card with the help of the stencil and embroider as shown.

62

MATERIALS

Papicolor card no. 41
Erica stencil no. 4050 312
White fine liner

Prick the pattern through the card with the help of the stencil. Draw the candles with the fine liner. Embroidery: bring the thread through the large hole and take the thread to the points as shown.

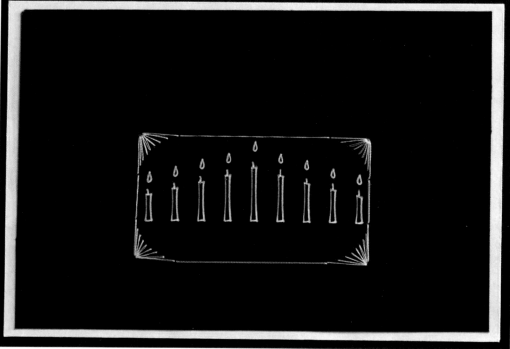

40

Congratulations

63

MATERIALS

Papicolor round card no. 41
Sheet no. 4050 953
Thread: Alcazar yellow

Embroidery: bring the thread through at 1 and take it to 2; go behind to 3 and take it to 4 and so on until the shape is complete. Cut the cake out and fix to the card with adhesive.

64

MATERIALS

Papicolor card no. 27
Thread: Alcazar metallic gold
3D sheet MB 9102

Embroider the scrolls in stem stitch. Attach the 3D picture.

65

MATERIALS

Papicolor card no. 27
3D sheet MB 9110
Thread: Alcazar soft green and blue; Reflecta gold

Embroider as follows: bring the thread through the large hole and take to the points as shown. Alternate blue and green each time. Outline the small squares with a stitch of Reflecta gold. Attach the 3D flowers.

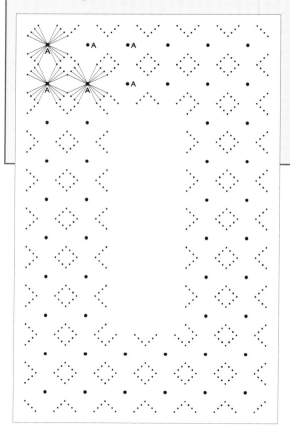

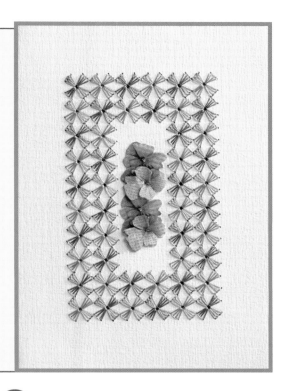

67

MATERIALS

Papicolor card no. 41
Thread: Alcazar metallic gold

Embroidery: see card 66. Make a pretty label or bookmark with the pattern.

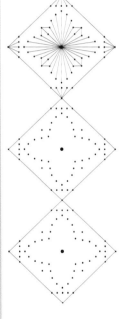

66

MATERIALS

Papicolor card no. 27
Erica stencil no. 4050 325

Prick the holes first and then do the embossing. Embroidery: bring the thread through the large hole and take to the points as shown. Outline the squares with a stitch of gold Reflecta.

68

MATERIALS

Papicolor card no. 27
Thread: Alcazar soft green
Silk ribbon: orange and
    yellow, and green for
    the bow

Embroider the border
and the stems with
stem stitch.
Flowers: push the
ribbon through the
card, make a knot and
push it through the
second hole.

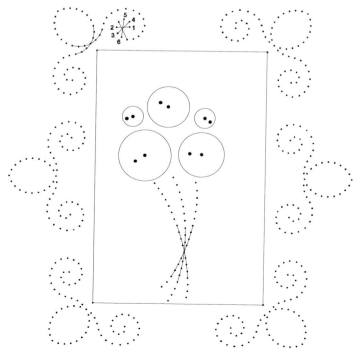

44

Sympathy

69

MATERIALS

Papicolor card no. 42
Thread: Alcazar metallic silver

Work the cross-stitches and outline the cross with a long stitch. Finish off the card with two strips of silver paper.

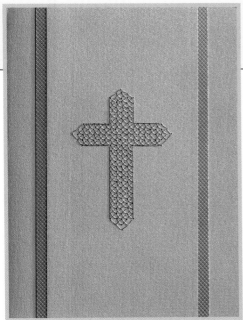

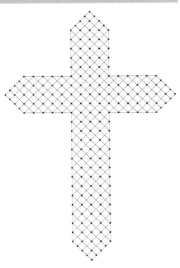

70

MATERIALS

Papicolor card no. 02
Erica stencil no. 4050 313
Thread: Alcazar metallic gold

Emboss the border then embroider the pattern in stem stitch.

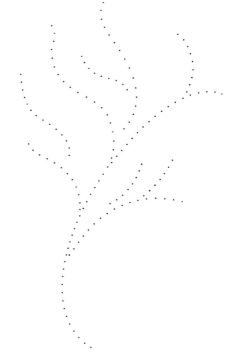

MATERIALS

Papicolor card Spectra no. 44
Thread: Alcazar light blue
Light blue silk ribbon

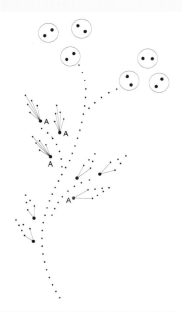

Embroider the stems in stem stitch. Leaves: bring the thread through the large hole and take to the points as shown. Silk ribbon: pull through the card to the front, make a knot (or two) in the ribbon and push the end through the other hole to the back.

72

MATERIALS

Papicolor card no. 27
Erica embroidery stencil no. 4050 338
Thread: Alcazar metallic gold

Draw a cross on the card using a ruler and pencil. Lay the stencil on it and prick the outer edge in each small square through the card. Repeat on the other side to form a cross. Choose scrolls to emboss in each corner.
Embroidery: bring the thread through from the back and take to the points as shown.

MATERIALS

Papicolor card no. 41
Thread: Alcazar metallic aqua

Straight lines: make straight stitches.
Curved lines: use stem stitch. The round
church window: bring the thread
through 1 and take to 2; go to 3 and
take thread to 4 and so on until the
circle is complete and there are two
strands in each hole.

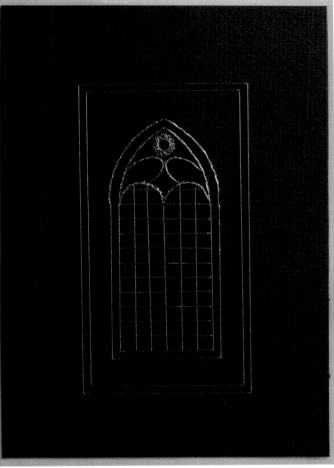

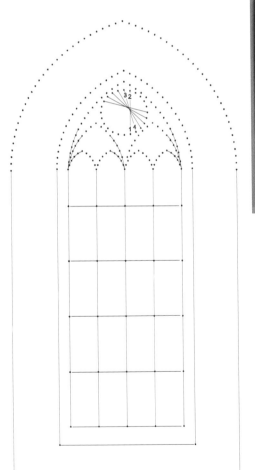

Picture Frames

74

MATERIALS

Papicolor card no.27
Thread: Alcazar blue/aqua and green

Embroidery: bring the thread through the large hole and take it to the points as shown. Complement the colours in the photo with the shades of thread you use.

A

75

MATERIALS

Papicolor card no. 27
Thread: Alcazar red and green

Instructions: see card no. 74.

76

MATERIALS

Papicolor card no. 42
Thread: Alcazar light blue

Embroidery: bring the
thread through 1 and
take it to 2; go behind
to 3 and take to 4 and
so on until you have
completed the shape.

Wreaths

77

MATERIALS

Papicolor card no. 10
Thread: Alcazar yellow and
soft green

Embroidery: Use the
coarse stylus to make sure
that the central hole is big
enough. Bring the thread
through the large hole
and take it to the points
as shown.

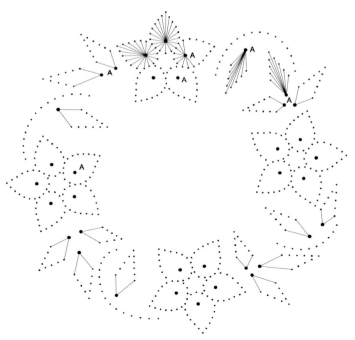

78

MATERIALS

Papicolor card no. 27, 8 x 8 cm (3 x 3 in)
Green paper
Silk ribbon: pale green and cream
Thread: Alcazar soft green

Embroider the leaves: bring the thread through the large hole and take the thread to the points as shown. Silk ribbon: bring through the hole from the back, make a knot and push ribbon through the second hole.

79

MATERIALS

Papicolor card pink no. 25

Instructions: see card no. 78. Secure each silk ribbon flower with a gold bead.

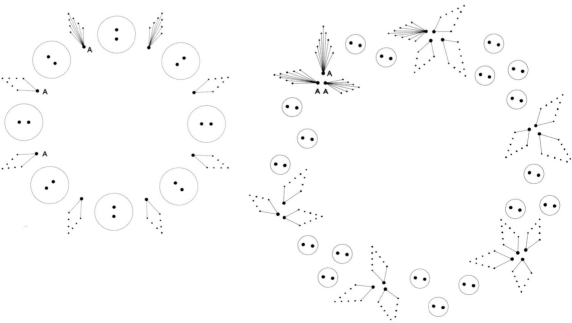

Wedding

MATERIALS

Papicolor card no. 19
Thread: Alcazar light blue, soft green and metallic gold

Embroidery: bring the thread through the large hole
and take it to the points as shown. Arch: use stem stitch.
Bells: bring the thread through 1 and take the thread
to 2; go behind to 3 and take the thread to 4 and so
on until you get to 1. Attach the photo with adhesive.

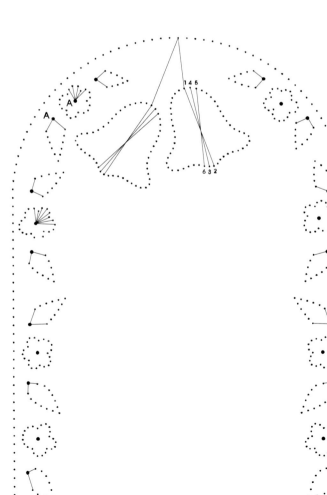

81

MATERIALS

Papicolor card
   no. 23
Gold paper
Thread: Alcazar
   metallic gold
Stencil no. 4050 304
Bead box no.
   4503 434

Prick the design
and then do the
embossing.
Embroidery: bring
the thread through
1 and take to 2; go
behind to 3 and
take the thread to
4 and so on until
the figure is
complete. Make a label and finish off the
card with a few pretty beads.

82

MATERIALS

Papicolor card no. 29
Thread: Alcazar soft green, pink and dark yellow

Embroidery:
bring the thread
through the large
hole and take it
to the points as
shown. Stems:
use stem stitch.

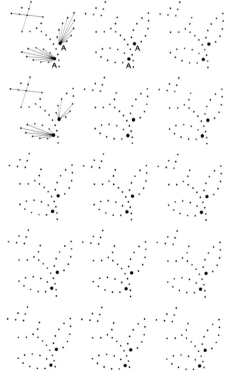

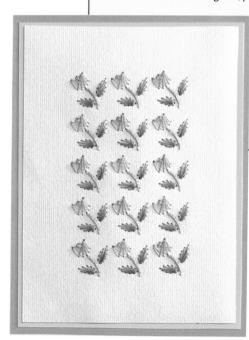

83

MATERIALS

Papicolor card no. 03
Thread: Alcazar metallic gold
Gold beads
3D step-by-step sheet no. 4008 098

Embroider the drops: bring the thread through
the large hole and take to the points as shown.
Work the border in stem stitch. Fix a bead in
each corner. Attach the 3D picture.

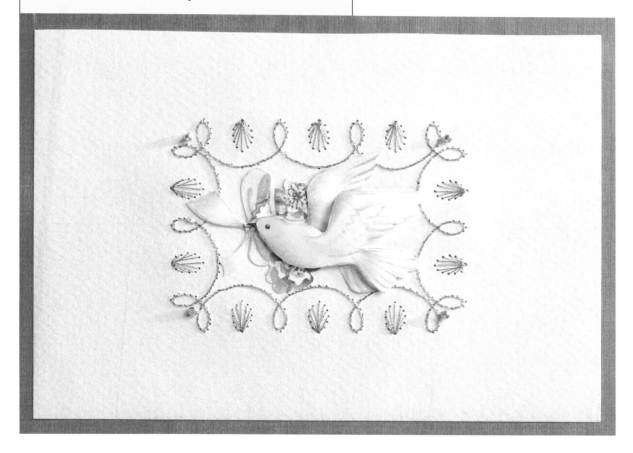

Retirement

84

MATERIALS

Papicolor card no. 25
Erica stencil no. 4050 304
Bead box no. 4503 436

Prick the design and then do the embossing.
Embroider the numerals in stem stitch. Put
the beads on a thread and attach it to the
inside of the double card.

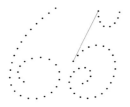

85

MATERIALS

Papicolor card no. 65
Erica geometric stencil no. 4050 301
Small gold beads
Thread: Reflecta gold

Prick the design and then do the embossing.
Embroider the numerals in stem stitch.
Attach the beads.

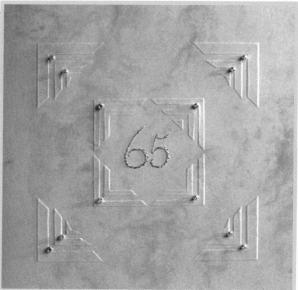

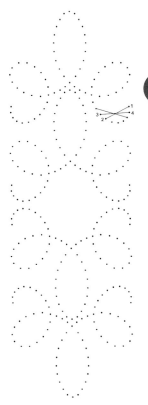

86

MATERIALS

Papicolor card
no. 44
Thread: Alcazar
metallic gold

Embroidery: bring
the thread through
at 1 and take it to
2; go behind to 3
and take the
thread to 4 and so
on until the figure
is complete.
Layer to make
a bookmark.

87

MATERIALS

Papicolor card no. 27
Erica embroidery template candlestick no. 4050 332

Find the middle line of the card by drawing
two intersecting lines using pencil and ruler
and place the stencil along it. After doing
the pricking, place the stencil on the other
side of the line to produce a mirror image.
Embroidery: follow the instructions on
the stencil.

88

MATERIALS

Erica embroidery set Spring no. 4050 114

Follow the instructions for the embroidery and attach the 3D picture.

89

MATERIALS

Erica candlestick embroidery template no. 4050 332
3D sheet MB 0010

Prick the corners of the template in the corners of the card and embroider following the instructions. Attach the 3D picture.

Rosettes

90

MATERIALS

Papicolor card Spectra no.37
Embossing stencil no. 4050 307
Thread: Alcazar mauve
Sparkles no. 4009 103

Prick the design then do the embossing.
Embroidery: bring the thread through at 1
and take it to 2; go behind to 3 and take the
thread to 4 and so on. Finish the card off
with six sparkles.

91

MATERIALS

Papicolor card no. 25
Thread: Alcazar pink
Embossing stencil no 4050 304
Sparkles no. 4009 103

Prick the design and then do the embossing.
Embroidery: see card no. 90.

92

MATERIALS

Papicolor card no. 03
Embossing stencil no. 4050 304
Sparkles no. 4009 111
Bead box no. 4503 436
Thread: Alcazar blue in 3 shades

Prick the design and then do the embossing. Embroidery: bring the thread through the large hole and take to the points as shown. Thread a number of beads on a coarse thread and secure the end of the thread to the inside of the card.

93

MATERIALS

Papicolor card no. 27
Embossing stencil no. 4050 303
Thread: Anchor Mouliné in 4 shades of yellow

Prick the design and then do the embossing. Embroidery: bring the thread through to 1 and take it to 2; go behind to 3 and take the thread to 4, and so on until each of the ovals is complete.

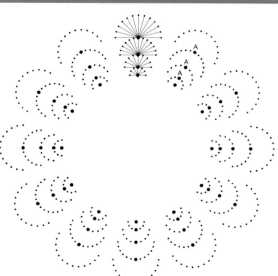

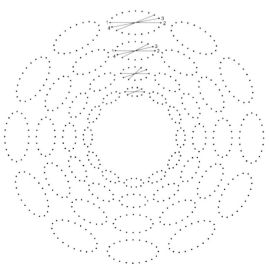

94

MATERIALS

Papicolor card Spectra no. 17
Thread: Alcazar metallic gold

Embroidery: bring the thread through at 1 and take to 2; go behind to 3 and take it to 4, and so on until the figure is complete.

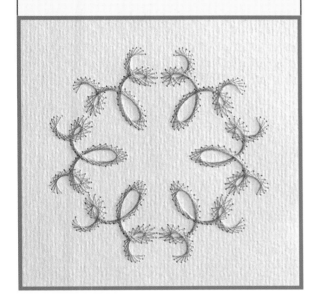

95

MATERIALS

Papicolor card no. 27
Thread: Alcazar soft green
Sparkles no. 4009 108

Embroider the leaves: bring the thread through the large hole and take it to the points as shown. Stems: use stem stitch.

Patchwork

96

MATERIALS

Papicolor card pink no. 25 and Spectra red no.12

Erica multi-stencil no. 4050 325

Paperpatch pink no. 4050 802

3D sheet MB 0009

Sticker border

Cut, emboss, and embroider the two figures above each other with the aid of the multi-stencil. Stick a strip of Paperpatch paper behind the opening. Attach the 3D sheet to the side of the card on the red strip. Stick the border on to the card.

97

MATERIALS

Papicolor card Spectra no. 19

Erica duck multi-stencil no. 4050 340

Paperpatch indigo no. 4050 810

Thread: Alcazar metallic gold

Prick, cut, and emboss the card with the aid of the multi-stencil. Embroider following the instructions. Fold strips of the Paperpatch paper, overlap and stick them down behind the opening.

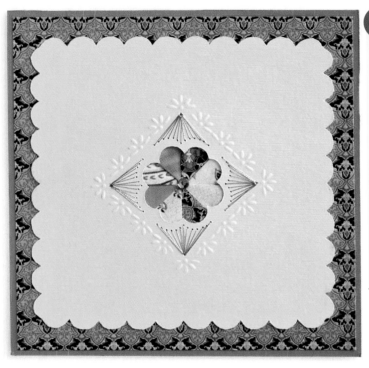

98

MATERIALS

Papicolor card no. 10
Erica multi-stencil heart no. 4050 339
Paperpatch yellow no. 4050 809
Thread: Alcazar metallic gold
Sparkles no. 4009 103

Prick, cut, and emboss the card with the aid of the multi-stencil. Embroidery: follow the instructions. Fold strips of the Paperpatch paper and starting from the centre overlap them in a circle behind the opening.

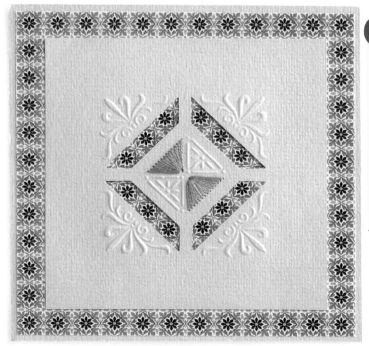

99

MATERIALS

Papicolor card no. 17
Erica multi-stencil no. 4050 326
Paperpatch block no. 4050 803

Cut, emboss, and prick the figure with the aid of the multi-stencil. Embroidery: see the instructions on the stencil. Stick a strip of Paperpatch paper behind the opening.

100

MATERIALS

Papicolor card no. 25
Erica multi-stencil no. 4050 324
Paperpatch pink no. 4050 802

Prick, cut, and emboss the figure with the aid of the multi-stencil. Embroider following the instructions. Stick different pieces of Paperpatch paper behind the openings.

101

MATERIALS

Papicolor card Spectra no. 42
Erica multi-stencil no. 4050 321
Paperpatch block no. 4050 803

Prick, cut, and emboss with the aid of the multi-stencil. Embroider following the instructions. Stick various pieces of Paperpatch paper behind the openings.

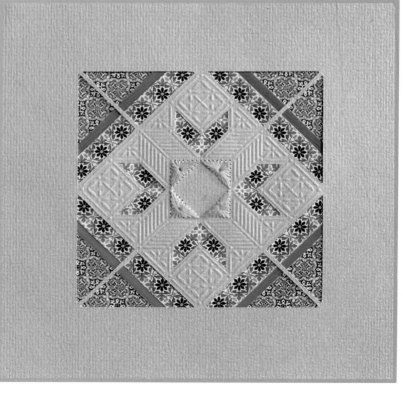